Chrysalis and Self

José A. Esparza Lozano

Examined Life Publishing

Printed in the United States of America

First Edition, 2019
ISBN: 978-1-7332853-0-8

www.josealanesparza.com

Chrysalis and Self

Lunch Poem #3

I just had lunch
And I am waiting for the bus.
I used to take the bus a lot when I was younger,
Although that was not too long ago.
The bridge looks beautiful to walk,
At this time of the day, circa 4,
The colors look surreal.
But I know as soon as I start walking
The shuttle will leave me behind,
Kinda like that one SpongeBob episode.
There is a girl in red,
She looks pretty and is the only one in the Lobby 7 pillars
      not wearing a black or dark blue jacket.

A moment of tension,
People are hurrying to cross Mass. Ave.,
The cars build up,
It's going to explode.
Then the light hits green
And everything smooths out.
The decay could merit it to be a Schwartz function.
When doing math I need motivation.
You often find it
In intangible applications.
Or is it in the abstract paintings?
The seeing the beauty of the small things,
Of this beautiful building.
I had never truly seen the green copper bars in the Lobby 7
      windows.
The shuttle is here.

Sleepwalk

A dream is work, is a flow, is a state of mind. The metric tensors of our thoughts diffuse as heat and fold just right. We change in proportion to our differences and behave by the dynamics of an ordered chaos, knowing only that entropy will remain and increase, but not if we will find peace.

We become crazy, anarchists, fall in and out of love. It is because of singularities that we know not if we can continue. Are we all that different? Or homeomorphically equivalent to a sphere? Holograms that become harder to understand when we live in fear. Holograms that become harder to understand the less we abstract and stay grounded to our three plus one dimensions that hurt, but at least exist. There are thoughts, there is rush, will I go for it, or only in my mind? Will the dreams happen, or will they fade? Will I acknowledge that everything was an impossibility and not even the sun was meant to be alive? They say "our chances really was a million to one", in a dream. I was always hoping I would change and become someone who could sing and dance, perform on a chalkboard for a wide audience, get the wows and the applause for the proof and be displayed like an animal in a zoo. How come I think of my goals but not of my mother every afternoon? Now my truth can only be reflected in my words, in what I write, for everyone wants the dream but no one really wants the life.

Whatever I do will fade away. The only thing I can hope for is enlightenment in a way. Bounce a photon or a drop, ripple the sea of life, and in that precious moment of truth become blind and never see again.

The behavior of how we bend, in space-time-metric-heat-like-flow, in heartache, in death of a loved, in the burn of how everything is really nothing and life will become a null, was always the voice telling us all along, that things were not that different from a sphere after all.

Coffee, Sunglasses, and the Empty Set

In the infinite but compact time that I have been alive
Today I walk floating around.
Today I am a pillar of salt.
Sometimes I feel a rush of blood
Of awe for humanity.
We can be immortal.
Vector bundles over manifolds are purple.
I love my family and don't want them to die.
My dogs will go first and that will also be a beautiful pain,
Reminiscence and heaven-like pain.

A room that seems like the Mind of god,
A complete Turing machine where everything is computable in
      polynomial time and much more,
And a human consciousness is a qubit,
Beyond existence, something I cannot conceive,
As impossible as smelling the colors of another person's mind.
I am still human, I still cry.
Because there is beauty in crying,
A climax of emotions about god, death, love, matter, the pain of
      the empty set,
The reassurance that something can come from nothing, at least
      in Peano's arithmetic, at least from being alive,
Or that math metaphors are as foolish as thinking we can be both
      dead and alive just because a function and its Fourier are
      not supported in the same domain.
I saw colors, I am never going to fail.
This little moment, this little line.
I wish I had a god to give glory to
In moments of full color.

I visit here to be redeemed and be calm,
Remind us that we are human and we need art.
We are afraid of the darkness.
We are at war.
And we fight for truth, in these walls, looking for the particle
      that will make us believe again.
Maybe humans are great, maybe we are pure, maybe there is
      more and more and more,

Than a hallway that seems infinite in sadness and life and joy
     and of people who are philosophical but only want to get
     tenure.
But it makes sense.
Because of moments like this.
Nothing else will matter but in beautiful and painful moments
     of colors and our families,
And our children and our love and our songs,
Because we long ago knew that a god particle will never come.

Purple Light

1. You are pure, bleach to my eyes, I want to drink you and balance the acid pouring in my blood.
2. I love people too much, that is why I hate the indifference of early April and the ignorance of an always today, in which Nazis and Commies are evil and we can solve quadratic polynomials, but I know nothing of deaths in Afghanistan and why there is a war.
3. The voice of a generation is someone you can relate in your angst, but is cool enough that you are not ashamed to admit that you are horny just like them, and want to blow your brains out just like them, and who you can give your attention and your adoration and they look like you.
4. I want time to stop,
But we made a deal,
For it to continue
And for me to forget
The pain in my muscles,
My back that I have to pull straight like a puppeteer or I look weak,
A frame I have to keep,
Concentration I have to give,
A world I have to ignore,
And exchange numbness for a lack of regret.
5. How can I focus in your eyes, and be cool, and in the colors that I used to live in under flashing lights, indie bands, myself, the sky, the books, and stories, and plots and conspiracy theories, and sincerely smiling continuously even in the hustle, if even the most simple conversations seem scripted to look as cool and as deep and as well read, and with good music taste, and not being humble.
6. It is in the chaos that there is a red maroon and a purple light to slow time and an aura.
7. Sometimes with rejection I find peace because at least I let a rush of adrenaline into my blood and whatever happens doesn't matter.
8. How deep can one mind go when it comes to the complexity of dealing with life, and feeling love for a person, and smiling, and tears that come with seeing your child born, or the fear of being attacked. How deep can one mind go for

leading others and being a martyr for a cause, marching, fighting, and never killing, but instead using the pen and the feet and the flesh and the blood of self, and the ambitions for wanting to make it into the top journals, and making money, and fucking all the people you always wanted to fuck, and being written of, and seeing a blue river and leafless trees, and the excitement of learning a new language if only at first, and smiling — truly smiling— those in which your eyes could cry as if they were being blown by a gust of wind, and you can feel euphoria in your chest and throat and even gut, and everything is okay, and there is food, or a joke. And how deep can a mind go when it comes to going to the depths of adventure, and the broadness of knowledge, and feeling pure. And how little of 100,000 when it comes to war, of those we don't know and choose to never know.

9. How hard is it to quit without grace, and instead go for the bang and the *buuurn*, and the I don't care I don't care I don't care, I never really cared, or perhaps less romantically I never knew I could.

10. Sometimes I want to stop being a person and just be a human, nameless, blank, however you cannot hide in your eyes, and in your hiding, and in your wrinkles, and in your muscles, and in your smile, and in your frown, and in your wanting for indifference, that this dream has been happening for as long...

11. Maybe with writing, and music, and connections, and noise, and love sounds, and love smiles, and tasty food and getting fucked up, and ecstasy and mushrooms will...

12. It's okay to eat animals, torture aside, as long as you kill them with love, and you are a just father who is doing it for the Good Cause. Of freedom and communism and equality and Kennedy and Castro?

13. Because the pain of an early April is felt when I lack, and am engulfed Chnd am not present, because what is not present is not, by definition. And what is outside is a fact. And I am a hip professional who is waiting to make it and break the barriers of the 2010s and I can't feel alone, and I should be proud to be an independent youth, and the song of drums and Sun and seeing your mother gone and the fire is an abstract, because fish have no feelings,

because they have always lived in water and never got to see the colorful Microsoft PC and Apple Macintosh.

14. We sometimes just want to connect, but at the same time we have a reality, for some reason, for some reason, and I can escape with books and with beer, and maybe it is not an escape after all because these things are what make life what it is, but somehow there are things that seem to stay and be unchangeable, and no one seems to be too worried about dying, but it would be weird if we all were, because maybe half of the people would romanticize getting a shotgun and putting it in your nose and then hearing a bang and then hearing no more.

15. But it's so hard to get off the script.

16. If I ignore your e-mails I am sorry everything is too much and I don't care too much to pretend.

17. Ignorance is bliss and I'm a fool for you.

No Peace *(Masters of War Revisited)*

We can romanticize the battles,
We can romanticize the pain,
But no one can love the fire from rain.

No one wins a war,
Our silence is sickening,
A Jesus complex,
My ignorance hurts.

I wished I knew more,
I wish I would read,
I wish I wasn't today
In which I feel weak.

I am not in rubble,
I am not in pain,
I have an anger,
But I can choose to abstain.
To forever ignore
The tears and the gore,
Shout for heroes and go.
You play with the love,
The land and the soil.

You cannot give your pride,
You cannot hold your frame.
Powerless in power,
What else do you want?
The battle with Battle can never be won.

The Lord is my shepherd,
A pasture of rubble,
The selling of feel,
Sometimes you can innocently kill.

Black Paper Flower Hanging Above

Take me back
To simpler times,
When words were winds,
Where we heard cries.
In an ever-today
The sounds we hear
Are not the gusts of else,
But what we make feel.

Take me forward, take me far,
Let me sleep today and feel numb.
In a Today I have to battle,
In a Today I feel dumb,
In kingdom come all pain is gone.

There is none to take me but time itself,
My feet, my hands, and mental realm.
A call to be awake,
A call to feel,
To let be,
And to see life for what it is.
A lot is in the past,
A lot of me is in the self,
A cloud comes
And I stop seeing the plants.
There is something about Today—
It is—
No need to believe.
Never be taken,
But by time.

Years of

It could be S^1,
A real domain with compact closure,
Or the set of points in the complex plane
Where iteration does not blow up whatever function
        defines us.
It forces us to act and to wait.
We could be watching the sunset,
But it is this not knowing that makes us run,
Chasing a sunset.
If you choose the world you live in
You can get there with walking,
And forever and simply see.
In question we live.
We can choose, but only to pretend.
A million truths we try to escape.
Sell the world and be above it
Or give it away.
A world that will always need pretending because
        we choose to,
But we are shaped from our always past.
In the bottom of the sea with no light,
And transparent souls,
And the earth shaking,
And everything that seems meaningless,
We came to be and somehow
We can give away the world.
There is not much to expect,
Knowing the stars in space,
The chaos we fear,
For good reason,
A healthy fear,
A sociopathy we are indoctrinated to ignore,
And indoctrinated to love the flash, the not changing,
        and the wanting for attention.
A long, long time ago.
We pretend to know,
Because ignorance hurts,
But it hurts more that we don't know
And feel or not in a higher above,

And I will never know what I will always miss,
By definition.
A celestial movement embedded in $\mathbf{R}^{3+1}$
That brings euphoria and washes the toxic if only for
       a moment,
If only forever.

Untitled #1

Those who in their life are human but nevertheless fight
To become monumental and greatest
And of pure mind,
Are forgotten.
For the world is too big and too full of stories and people
To remember all.
There is a war for our attention,
The wavelengths and focus of your brain,
The capacity that all the past has given us,
To truly stop,
Think, be, and create.

'Cause there's not
Many men that've done the things that you've done,
And everything you've pushed yourself to be,
And all the fighting, and the reading
Keeps my head unbowed.

The sea roars for what is has seen.
There's a million races being run.
And you can try your best and still lose the war
And have your name be hated on,
Doused in mud,
Without god and without money,
Not being able to go home.

Whatever needs to be done.
There is a life in fear
Becoming a killer.
History will forgive us,
Whoever controls the chaos,
And whoever wins the war.

In the fighting,
We are all brothers when we are betrayed.
We are imperfect and cause the splatter of blood,
Or the pressure and the anger and pain.
Maybe if we could, we would heal everyone,
But our memory will be shattered,
And in time,

Whatever awe we felt
Will be the spit with which others their metal will shine.
As soon as we open our mouth
We risk,
For we have created a dichotomy where we are bound to
        exist.
When we both don't know,
Yet stick to our faith,
Spit will be splattered
In the mountain of your name.

The Unions and Intersections of Thoughts and People

A plant that needs sun,
A computer that breathes.
In each of the moments in which we became lost or so we
      thought,
And the mind you have to regain,
And the solutions to our biology.
Many things would be different if I went back in time.
It is easy to justify the present and want to never regret,
The moments and decisions we lived in life and the counter-
      factuals will never be seen.
Your brain is trained to forget when you sleep.
And we are shaped in a way that we want.
But the choices that make us and shape us,
And control us, is a dynamic process
That iterates and iterates,
Leaving a discontinuous fractal
Of possibilities,
Made and undone,
And thought of, and could have been spin-offs,
A trace that cannot be relived,
And whatever mark that is left,
Of the thoughts and our moments,
And all that we gave,
The music notes and tones that floated in our brain,
And the subatomic particle we left an imprint on,
An inconceivable but well defined shape,
And its topology,
And all the information.
A computer that breathes,
A plant that needs sun.
All the vectors that we in some way got to be,
And blood flow that combined with society laws,
Led us to rivers,
And a flow of whatever,
The prayer meditated by a drop of water,
And the imprint of electrons, bits, ink, and paper.

Green Tranquility 167

When they tell you it's nothing
Is when you most want to know.
In days like this, in days in which the sky is blue, and not
        precisely gray,
And the internet is out and there is nothing there for you to
        stay,
And you grab the pen or the keyboard and start to type for
        fifteen minutes,
It is easy to remember that I am able to create.
It is easy to see a show or read, history and fiction,
But living life as an observer is the worst curse I can let
        myself be.
People spend their lifeblood to keep me entertained,
And my eyes following a distinct motion,
A same pattern of light,
That changes the chemical flow in the blood of your brain,
That makes us love a lie.

When you are also a creator,
Or so you think,
You can then appreciate
The writing of others like a brother,
Dreaming of drinking the nectar in Olympus,
In a way, or you'll see if you wait,
But the life that we say we will live,
Will only very conditionally come.
Breathing the lines,
Seeing eye to eye with an artist,
There is no reason not to,
For we both have a brain.
Who gets to be a genius?
Is it the ones who won a revolution and fought the night?
Is it the ones who were able to people unite?
Who know our emotions and strike a perfect chord,
Saying the same things we are feeling, but
Unlike us they are able to find the words,
And the notes and the lights,
And running away.

Everything is always written in a rush.
The slowest pen strokes, which require many thoughts,
Are a projection of the infinite dimensional vector spaces
Created by our finite neurons,
Clash and exploration, exclamation.
And the voices of other friends,
The rhythms that combine with beauty to create the one-in-
      a-million.
Writing for those moments first and listening to the more,
The tranquility that is in the base of our beat,
That drives the oxygen and makes your veins expand.

Being driven, all that you live always integrates to this,
All the nights walking alone,
Motivated by the illusion of something not present,
Ignoring the reality,
And all the dawns of epiphany and illumination,
And the impulses of your nerves, that create through a
      network
Of electric potential in a discrete set,
Combine to make a sparking moment
That changes the color of your soul.
A dark purple light which turns into a red surrounded by
      black,
In which in the blue notes
Everything culminates.
And on a path that we all path,
And we are afraid we will not return,
In a room of your friends you listen to your words,
A room that will soon be empty,
And then by yourself.
And in these moments we are condemned
To what is our birthright—
Standing alone in a moment of blind.
It feels repeated and it will always return as the sun.
The jump that brought a challenge,
The speed that we needed to gain,
And the moment in which we become and let what makes
      us thus speak,
Is a voice not to be lost until the last day.

A Letter to —

Today I had a dream in which I was in an old and perhaps never existing flying carrier, a combination of a wooden ship and floating balloon characterized by a large open view of what is ahead. This carrier experienced turbulence, as many of our souls, and in the escalation of chaotic motion we began to fall. We hit the ground, and unrealistically I didn't die on impact. I was on the floor, everything felt as something I wasn't in control of. I was unconsciously trying to stand up as the images of trees and concrete were fading away as with what I can only think dying must be. There is no point in panicking, and I am talking to myself as my body is instinctively and automatically trying to stand up and my mind is just observing these last moments of life.

As with many times before, as I experience my last moment of life, something not less than a miracle occurs which is that I am given another chance of continuing to live, in the form of waking up to the world which we both experience. I wish I could say that I learned from dying without being dead and analyzed my last thoughts and in those last moments of colors before infinite emptiness see what I truly love, fear, and regret. Perhaps I am a little wiser than who I was yesterday, in this knot of space and time in which we only move forward, but from yesterday things overall have not changed. Everything turned to a memory, and as I lived my day, and joked with friends, and learned and read more, and ate, these deep loves, fears, and regrets became lateral to my immediate consciousness, or perhaps another small component in which my mind embeds into. In any way, it's to soon to say, perhaps I'll have a dream today. And whatever it shows, and the seeds that from it grow, will prepare me for when the fall comes my way.

Chalk Poem #1: Camera

In a snapshot projecting our feelings,
To a time and from an image-moment
Of what is never to be seen in the exact same
       configuration
Despite the stillness of all
The unchanging tendencies and canon of nature,
Constant as through our perception of Noetherian
       symmetries—
Capturing light and time
And the chromatism
Existing in the grey matter of ourselves.

John Nash v. Bobby Fischer

A game of chess, moving the pieces and strengths,
Managing the what-ifs and possibilities,
As time is slow,
Yet played in blitz.
Openings and canon,
The lessons from the past,
And the lives of people gone
We ought to analyze,
And mistakes and moments.
As if this all could
Make us reach perfection
Like no one else has.

An immortal match,
A vacuous truth
As with everything,
Is after the moment dead
And in our memory alive.

Nevertheless, the getting away
Of structure and its always decay
Leads to staying moments of clever,
Remaining only in what we see.
An end being perpetuated.
A feel in the air.
Is the novelty in the beginning
The innocence of all?
Or is it in the moment we jump forward,
When knowing we could fall?
As every time we play it's a new day.
A sun has risen to bless and to pray,
A sun that has been god, devil, fire, and clouds
Forming from the geodesic attraction
From a non-empty darkness and playground of nature—
A mirror where we can see how big and how small
At the same time all is, and nothing at all.
And that all in all creates sunrises,
A local property encapsulated
In what looks like an infinite, yet within

An epsilon in a manifold.

The earth also rises.
We breathe
And forget our hallucinations and dreams.
Life is rhythmic and harmonic,
Encapsulating the periodic.
Another reason to
Not stop and for not giving up.
As the chaos of the endgame,
And taming a moment,
And keeping our frame,
Is the only reward for living the game.
And even with growth in the loss,
What do we gain?
A question and answer
Forever in the fabric with
Which our eyes can see the reflection,
And pluck to see all that is Being.
As the day and night
Are positions
Felt in an epsilon radius of light.

Chalk Poem #2: Fall

There was this year the autumn
That in its first days we could see
A contrast of fire in trees
And a colorless sky as a pond.
And I realized
I had never looked closely at autumn.

Many of the leaves have fallen
And what remains is a raw
Dark wooden foundation—
Stillness—
And branches as nerves.

And the coming of season
Seems to match
The time and the audience of its people.

Chalk Poem #3: Sleep

Sometimes in those moments,
About to sleep or awake,
There's an in between state in which some unknown set
      of molecules show me truth and hallucination—
A feeling that life is a Dirac distribution
And every moment awake
Is everything and absolute and there is none outside
But suffocation of time,
And being alive is to breathe.
And seeing the nothingness beyond the day to seize
Will gift you pain and truth and haste.
And existence is the empty trying to cry—
There are no possessions, only illusions and what we
      occupy.

Airport Poem #1

I just arrived from a plane
And I am waiting for my brother.
He was suppose to be here earlier,
But that is okay.
And even if he is late,
Does he not love me?
Are we not part of those for who we are willing to kill and die?
Will he see my children as part of him?
And all we have lived?
And all the moments that we passed together,
Seen by no one but ourselves and that will never be seen again,
And the advice in our adulthood,
And all that I learned,
And all the time I never realized
An emptiness that is not perceived nor admitted
Because neither of us is dead yet.

Is death also my brother I wonder?
We will be together forever
And is always in my mind.
I see people who don't seem to be particularly thinking of
        death right now.
They are hugging and are happy,
And remember each other's behaviors,
And how we say hi.
It makes me think of all the times I've been a dick,
To my family and to those I love,
And to myself,
Letting me not experience
The pleasures of patience and of listening to others in the
        manner of Atlas.
For listening is a craft and something to carry,
And true art hurts,
As much as the thought that we are mere mortals, and this
        thought itself gives us life.

And as I write this I am still waiting
For one of my brothers to come.

Humans and Trees

I have things to do and a task
And I don't do them,
But I only have to do them for myself.
And as long as my mother still loves me perhaps I am not
      fucking up too much.
Artificial effort that has to be put to maintain and to keep,
And to live life without leaving something to be desired,
      And not something to wish for.
We all go crazy and get different chances.
The intentions and emotions
And life and everything was just an accident.
And hopefully the people around you understand,
Since we are all in this same ship, and someday if we are
      true,
Will have to face the challenge of having to see the un-
      known,
And a painful ignorance and uncertainty.
Or perhaps not.

Looking through the mirror you see the eyes
Of every one of your ancestors
And how they shaped you,
And the monkeys and the trees where we come from,
All made human.
All the crying and all the blood,
And the laughing, and seeing someone who you had wanted
      to see for a long time and you thought they were
      gone
Are emotions and moments embedded in the canon
Of what is never written but always told.
They were never lying.
You know children come from mothers,
And that everyone grows,
And the years pass—
At first without much thought—
And it was never a lie to see everyone and everything
      change.

Creativity of the Mango

The ideas and the times
Shown and discovered
And created and fought for forever,
Or is it in being in love?
With the art and the process?
Da Vinci left paintings incomplete.

Giving your life and soul and devotion
And fighting a war, the genius of Pancho Villa and Jean
      Bourgain,
And the revolutionary movement and death.
When is killing not a murder?
What are the problems of our time?
Should a composer abandon music
And use their brain to many lives save?
Or do you have to be in love
With greatness and the feeling of awe?
Or would everything be better and pure if this is some-
      thing I ignore?
And be a lake and sun and lepton,
And see that we are not apart from nature,
And black holes.
And if we are so, then in discovery we are knowing
      ourselves,
And the fucking amazing interactions that lead to us
      and this—
An 11th dimensional TV,
A puppeteer show alive through strings.

The Present and the Elsewhere

Sometimes I think of the greatness I can achieve,
The aspects of the world that I can change,
And the visions I can see.
Of putting the labor and all the memories of the past
To build and fight for an altruistic legacy to surpass,
To let everyday be moments of glory,
And every breathing second a moment of thanks,
And use all my clarity and focus and brain cells
To not let life waste behind.

And sometimes I feel like a waste,
As if all I can ever hope for is to end this phase
And admit the defeat that is to come,
And be mindful there is a probability that I won't live past
        my youth—
See the irony of having had dreams,
And regret having let my mind spend so much time in the
        elsewhere and the past.

To sport death.
The journey is every day written, and the path I don't know.
And when I forget I have worth I remember in moments of
        flow,
And focus and pain,
All the essence of the brain.
We are all and only our minds.
For we will feel pain one way,
In the present or in regret,
The transformation of a conserved quantity,
And the beauty in chaos and fractals of life-dynamics,
That is deterministic yet but the iterations of its fundamen-
        tals.

To dream is to be is to create.
And seeing how time is passing and makes no mistakes
Is sad and beautiful and gives a smile and a tear.
Once you are dead there is nothing to fear.

Opportunities that Come and Go

It is difficult so see and conceive
The mentality to be able to believe
And breathe the essence of this room.
The day and sky of three suns
And the trajectory and spinning in space we seem to
        ignore.
Constellations and trees are both from nature,
And the seemingly infinite distance
Is coexisting through the minds
Of monkeys reading and writing,
And the drums and tones
That come natural and both seem theoretical—
Harmonic and in different manifestations.

We can improve and stand for the call
Of moments or of duty.
And it is astonishing how easy it is to forget
Details and conversations we had engaged in
And enjoyed
And had only been in a moment ago.
Although it is more astonishing
All the memories that do stay,
And the way it all accumulates.

Many times before, I daydreamed
About what life would be like at my current age.

The Language of Doing

1. I am hoping to get to be myself.
I think of myself as what I do, and mostly only the positive things I
     keep.
I am somewhat happy of my mistakes.
It is easy to say that.

2. Sometimes when something horrible happens
I don't particularly care,
Or I laugh.
And I wonder if I am going to hell because of this,
Since more than showing what I do,
Which I try to do altruistic things,
I reveal my sociopath tendencies
And all the egocentrism and evil inside me,
And maybe my six-year-old self would be disappointed.

3. When I am walking in the street I sometimes pick up trash that I
     see,
It is something good for the world and more people should do it.
And I don't do it for the looks but I am aware it looks different in a
     good way,
At least a girl once said that to me,
And there is a reason I copied it from an old friend
That I don't talk to anymore,
And I think is doing a lot of drugs now,
Although that is not the reason we are not talking.

4. I took too much caffeine today.
I say the word 'flow' a lot in my poems because I want to improve
     my attention,
Which is not a terrible thing.
But I have been sabotaging my own happiness in many ways,
But that is also normal for people to do.

5. I am trying to ascend
To a state of mind in which I can control my thoughts and not be
     distracted by stupid shit,
Like lovers that never became true,
And debates I have in my mind while talking to myself,
Trying to justify to the world the decisions I make,

And that I am not an immoral person for not being perfect.
But since I am just talking to myself, I am actually just being very
    stupid about how I spend my time.

6. I don't think I have very good music taste.
After a session of watching stupid videos of people getting knocked
    out in street fights,
And 'To Catch a Predator' and snippets of 'Curb Your Enthusiasm',
Both psychological masterpieces by the way,
My head hurts.
The former show is a little fucked up and somewhat immoral to
    produce in my opinion,
But it is already out there so we might as well enjoy the shaming
    of others and study the psychological profiles of people that
    have actually fucked up their lives.
It makes me feel that I haven't fucked up too much myself just
    because I don't focus enough on my homework;
And it is exactly these types of thoughts that make me think I might
    go to hell,
But I stopped believing in hell and the devil a long time ago, before I
    stopped believing in god.

7. In my adult life I learned that organized Satanists are actually
    atheist who are being ironic,
And I think that is funny.
I always knew that Satanists are not bad people,
And by always I mean around age 12 or so when my older metalhead
    cousin had started reading the Satanic Bible
And I could see that it was not that bad,
But my parents still take many of these things literally,
And that is okay.

8. The first time I dreaded about the emptiness of the universe was
    when I learned that it is likely that everything will cool off
    and nothing will be left but light traveling in empty space,
Everything either sucked by black holes
Or so cold that nothing is moving.
I don't know if that is scientifically accurate,
But it can be daunting to hear when you are young.

9. I think it is healthy to have a deep existential crisis when you are
    14 or 15.

At the moment it obviously sucks,
And the feeling of nothingness and emptiness of life will never go
      away,
But as later in life the people around you start feeling the same
You have had more time to think of these things and you can also
      empathize and relate.
You can still be happy if you are a nihilist.

10. Today I was tearing a little at the thought of people I love dying,
I find it healthy, and it happens at the most unexpected moments.
I'd rather cry and reevaluate the way I behave while they are alive.
I haven't done anything terrible to make me deeply regret my life
      choices,
And I am still young,
But if I don't constantly remind myself of the possibilities that life
      can be,
Both in the love I can give to others and in general,
I might live a life short of what I can truly achieve.
And that will probably be very sad,
And perhaps even a waste to be honest.
Although it is weird since at the end of the day we are just ants
Floating in space.
So the mere fact that we can try to be happy, and calm our sense of
      self-importance,
Is the same as any other life you can choose.
But then I think again and there is a particular type of happiness,
And dopamine, serotonin, and adrenaline mix,
That comes with victory.

11. I was surprised that they played "We Are The Champions" when
      France won the World Cup this last summer.
I thought it was a little cliché,
But then again we are all archetypes.
And I'm sure that when you are holding the World Cup
The song playing in the background is the last thing you care about.

Nature

They say humans did not invent fire,
But fire invented humans,
As it nourished our brain
Forcing us to become geniuses not in desire but for
      survival
In a ruthless nature that destroys as much as it creates.

We were born out of genocide,
Killing every other species that looked like us
Until only we remained,
King of all apes,
And of this earth,
Speaking in extinct languages
Stories that are never to be heard.

Finding Flowers

Today the sun is out,
The ice in the river is melting,
And is a beautiful moment
In which I am alive,
And not in doubt about happiness today and to come,
And glad I get to see and meet
Monsters and giants
Who have pathed the way of knowledge.
I wonder what it must feel in his age?
All the legends he met and lived,
And the theorems in his name.
The pureness of giving all you can in consistence
Is the basis for the beauty and elegance and style that
    shows.

It is from conversations that I've learned the most in
    life,
From sporadic questions and comments
Whose answers have stayed like music notes.

I see a life
And a tranquility that can be fulfilled,
And I can only but hear
About the practices and battles alone.

Wave Equation

The lines between which we write,
Bend and curve and hallucinate,
Existing trough descriptions,
In its self-essence,
In our minds,
And as the observables of
What comes from the sun,
And what we experience and love—
Visions and sounds
Of people you miss.
Water is transparent so that as fish
We can see the god-given gift of light.

I hear the voice of my grandmother on the phone,
A voice that has cried for the death of a son
But is now speaking to me after my age has come.
It means more than words,
And yesterday I was a kid,
And I haven't changed fundamentally as a person,
I keep the same name and personality
And have not lost the sense of me,
But yet the time is
In which there are no more dreams but plans,
And a fight against entropy
For our configuration to be.

The defining factor in transition,
Beyond maturity and skill set, to truly draw the line,
Is to live by the words
No more wasting time,
No more wasting time,
No more wasting time.

Manywhere

We hesitate to be free
Because we don't know what it truly looks like
And can only imagine.
Quaternions are every day in our life
Connecting and creating,
Summing to all that can be described.

The opposite of memories
Is painting times to come.
And in the same way our mind can play us
To remember non-existent moments
And either numb or romanticize the past,
What is ahead is a function of what we think,
And of a brain of flesh and carbon
That you can choose to command.

Observation is creation
When you let your mind see what no one else has.

The Social and Algebraic Animal

Life is strange. We live and have a structure and a face, and everything seems ordered since everything we are is a consequence and the sum of how we act, but existence is feeble and an instant, and life is very trippy as a whole. We are primates, but we are these beings with an identity that follows us. And we are in space and we all like something called art and parties for good reasons, precisely because it is an instant.

The cycle will never end and I have to learn to either love what I do or do things that I love, or a linear combination of both.

Some Human Emotions

Fear that overrides all your strength, making you ask for help
as the child we all were, knowing there is nothing that
can be done once you hear the gun, and being angry
and crying thinking your brother is gone.

Indifference about all that never mattered and cynicism, hav-
ing in the back of your mind the knowledge that you
are a human with cancer, and that none can under-
stand the weight and the mundane, and that this is an
injustice, and all your abstract dreams are gone, and
in our last times we only have family.

Believing that you are in love because you are lonely.

Endurance of forcing yourself to practice your skills for a
consistent uninterrupted time aside, and your brain
sparking, making the connections and leaps, being an
athlete. What I want is possible. I am a champion in
my mind.

Disrespected, wishing you were stronger, and being reminded
that you are a monkey that has the devil's type of
pride.

Remembering that we are all consciousnesses and minds,
and that the one-dimensional first person view of the
world is the same that everyone else is having and the
same class of experience that every human who has
existed and died has had.

Chalk Poem #4: Eventually Zero Sequences

The concept of a life, beyond the self,
Includes the walks
And the colors and sounds of birds and trees,
The surroundings that we can experience and share,
Beyond the individual and the continuum of time.
Touch is the existence of the sensation and the object.
We will never know if things are still real after we die.

Mirror Symmetry

I had a déjà vu
Of seeing us all being in the same room,
A specific oddity,
A configuration I think I dreamt but didn't imagine
        to occur.
The simplest words are
Knowledge nested and nested.
It burns to see we are the same age,
And the gap doesn't make me envy
But be inspired,
A cleansing fire making me desire
Authenticity to breathe and speak the language
And what is not impossible to reach.
The elasticity of words,
Of the non-commutative,
Of what was played with from the cradle—
Art we cannot observe.
Euler's blindness didn't matter when his craft lived
        in his mind.
How much is creation,
And how much do we find?
Extensions and deformations,
The affine and the divine.
Concretely meditating in the simple,
Witnessing beyond colors,
Elevating,
To live for and in truth,
Seeking the uncertainty of uncertainty.

NOTES

The cover image is of a sphere filling curve. It appears in "Hyperbolic Structures in 3-manifolds, II" by William P. Thurston.

Lunch Poem #3

Schwartz functions are a type of infinitely differentiable functions in mathematics that decay to zero faster than any inverse polynomial, and for which all of its derivatives also decay faster than any inverse polynomial. For example, the function $f(x) = e^{-x^2}$ is a Schwartz function.

Sleepwalk

The Ricci flow is a type of mathematical process by which an abstract geometrical shape, a manifold, can be smoothed out through dynamics analogous to the flow of heat. Grigori Perelman in 2002 and 2003 provided a solution to the Poincairé conjecture via advances of our understanding of the Ricci flow. The Poincairé conjecture, now a solved theorem, states that all simply connected and closed three-dimensional manifolds are homeomorphic to a three-dimensional sphere. The Generalized Poincaré conjecture was proved for dimensions greater than or equal to five by Stephen Smale in 1961, and for dimension four by Michael Freedman in 1982.

Coffee, Sunglasses, and the Empty Set

Whether if the solution to a problem can be *verified* to be correct or not by a computer 'quickly' then necessarily implies that the problem can be *solved* 'quickly', is the classic P vs NP problem, which remains unsolved.

Peano's arithmetic is the standard way to set up the logical foundation for the natural numbers $\mathbf{N} = \{0, 1, 2, 3, \dots\}$ and its arithmetic via an abstract construction of numbers relying almost only on empty sets as the building blocks and axioms on how these constructions behave.

The well-known Schrödinger's cat paradox is a thought experiment formulated by Erwin Schrödinger that depends on the Heisenberg uncertainty principle. The Heisenberg uncertainty principle, while having a physics interpretation, can be purely formulated as a principle of harmonic analysis— that a function and its Fourier transform cannot both be supported in "small domains", that is, if one is very concentrated the other has to be very spread out.

Years of

Dynamical systems, chaos theory, and complex analysis are the mathematical areas that most deal with fractals. Most commonly recognized fractals are constructed as, or are closely related to, the set of points in the complex plane (imaginary numbers) such that evaluating a function on a point and then on its subsequent output, and so on iterating forever, leads to a bounded stable number rather than blowing up. S^1 is a symbol to represent the one-dimensional sphere, i.e. a circle, and $\mathbf{R}^{3+1}$ is a symbol to represent three dimensions of space and one of time.

Chalk Poem #1

Noether's theorem, by Emmy Noether, roughly states that for every symmetry in a physical model of nature there is a corresponding conservation law. Two examples of this correspondence are that if you assume the laws of the universe are the same in all points in space, then this implies the conservation of momentum in the universe, and if you assume the laws of the universe have been and will be the same across all time, then this implies the famous conservation of energy in the universe.

Chalk Poem #3

The Dirac distribution $\delta(x)$, often written as the 'Dirac delta function', is a function used in physics such that

$$\delta(x) = \begin{cases} +\infty & \text{when } x = 0, \\ 0 & \text{when } x \neq 0, \end{cases}$$

and with the property that $\int_{-\infty}^{\infty} \delta(x)dx = 1$. It is used to model the density of a point-mass or a point-charge in space. It is not a true function in the formal mathematical sense, but it can be formalized through the theory of distributions pioneered by Laurent Schwartz.

The Present and the Elsewhere

In special relativity, given a starting point in space-time (x_0, t_0), the *future* describes the points in space-time that can be reached by information from (x_0, t_0) traveling at the speed of light, this *future* in turn becomes the points where there can be an effect from (x_0, t_0). The *past* is the collection of points in space-time for which (x_0, t_0) is in their *future*. The *elsewhere* is the collection of points in space-time that are far enough in

space and time such that information sent from the *elsewhere*, even at
the speed of light, cannot reach (x_0, t_0). This means that points in the
elsewhere cannot have a cause-and-effect relation with (x_0, t_0). For exam-
ple, if our starting point in 1+1 dimensional space-time is $(x_0, t_0) = (0,0)$
and c is the speed of light, then the collection of points inside the cone
created by the lines $(\pm ct, t)$ for $t > 0$ is the *future*, the collection of points
inside the cone for $t < 0$ is the *past*, the collection of points exactly in
the lines is the *present*, and points outside of the cones are in the *elsewhere*.

For example, the distance between the Sun and the Earth is about 150
million kilometers, and with the speed of light being about 300 million
meters per second, then light from the Sun takes about 500 seconds to
reach the Earth. This means that given a specific light signal from the
Sun, the Earth is in the *elsewhere* with respect to the origin of the signal
for the first 499 seconds after it is sent. After that, there is enough time
for the information to reach us and we are in the *present* at the 500 second
mark, and in the *future* any time after that.

Nature

See Suzana Herculano-Houzel's talk "What is so special about the hu-
man brain?".

Wave Equation

The wave equation is a partial differential equation that describes the
behavior of any wave: sound, electromagnetic, gravitational, etc. For
example, if the displacement of a point in a wave in $n + 1$ dimensional
space-time is given by the function $u(x, t)$, then the motion of the wave
can be described by the homogeneous wave equation

$$\partial_t u(x, t) = \Delta u(x, t).$$

Manywhere

Quaternions are a generalization of imaginary numbers first described
by William Rowan Hamilton. Similarly to how imaginary/complex
numbers are a two-dimensional extension of the real numbers and con-
structed by adjoining an element i such that $i^2 = -1$, quaternions are a
four-dimensional generalization of the real numbers where we adjoin
elements i, j, k such that $i^2 = j^2 = k^2 = ijk = -1$.

ACKNOWLEDGEMENTS

First and foremost, I want to thank Ed Barrett for being a great teacher and an inspiring mentor. I thank the participants of the MIT Spring 2018 Poetry Workshop. I also thank Susan Carlisle and Ken Urban from whom I learned a lot. I am deeply grateful to Jade Coulin, Sergio Dominguez, Zoya Fan, George Friedlander, Wei Xun He, and Artemisia Luk who all in some way influenced this book.

I thank Valorie K. Ruiz for her mindful editing.

I am especially thankful to my brothers Beto and Jorge, and my cousins Manny, Kuko, and Cesar with whom I learned how to freestyle rap, along with many other things in life.

Finally, I thank my parents Aída Argelia and José Alberto, my grandmothers Amalia and Emma, and my aunts Chiquis and Vira.

Made in the USA
Monee, IL
07 July 2026

56553294R00031